THE CATR THEORY™

The 4 Legs of Successful
Personal and Professional
Relationships.
It's NOT Rocket Science!
(CATR: pronounced 'cater')

Laurie Thibert

Dedication

Dearest Osei,

The *gift of YOU* in my life and our world is priceless.

I am so grateful we get to grow in partnership

and help others succeed in theirs.

Much love and respect always,

Mom

Contents

Preface

Our world is struggling! Big time!

We seem to have lost the ability to connect with one another to create long-lasting, high-quality relationships. The relationships we have, whether personal or professional, break down at times, and we often don't know how to repair them.

Each day is a roller coaster of difficult situations and the intense emotions that come with them.

Misunderstandings, unmet expectations, broken trust, and disrespect, which often begin as minor issues, can quickly evolve into significant problems when left unaddressed or handled in unhealthy ways.

Before you know it, those involved have become upset and divided. Instead of coming together in partnership to overcome life's challenges and experience more connection and joy, there's bitterness, resentment, and division.

A significant amount of research indicates that high-quality relationships, both in personal life and at work, are key to achieving happiness. Understanding how to foster healthier relationships in all areas of our lives will make a big difference in our overall happiness.

What if relationships aren't as complicated as they seem to be?

What if there is a way to look at relationships through a filter that could help you clearly see which piece of the puzzle is at play and how to fix it?

Hi, I'm Laurie. With decades of experience as a relationship development specialist, I'm here to offer insights to help you increase your Relational Intelligence (known as RQ) to create GREAT relationships and experience more joy and happiness with the people you care about.

What is Relational Intelligence (RQ)?

Relational Intelligence, or RQ, is a relatively new area of study.

Relational Intelligence (RQ) is both the capacity and capability to create, nurture, and sustain high-quality connections. It reflects how effectively a person understands, navigates, and elevates relationships— especially in complex environments.

High-RQ leaders build trust quickly, communicate with clarity, repair conflicts proactively, and create conditions where people feel valued, heard, and energized.

In the context of **high-quality connections**, RQ is what enables:

- **Authentic communication** that strengthens understanding
- **Mutual trust and psychological safety**
- **Accountability that fosters respect**
- **Positive interaction patterns** that increase engagement and collaboration

High-RQ isn't just about being good with people—it's about intentionally cultivating relationships that drive well-being, performance, and sustainable success.

The CATR Theory™ encompasses the qualities needed for High-Relational Intelligence (High-RQ) interactions that support healthy, fulfilling relationships.

Here is the most significant insight of all:

Relationships don't have to be hard!

While they can be very challenging at times, (especially in today's world), contrary to popular belief, relationships do not have to be as difficult as we often make them.

Most relationships are relatively simple once we recognize the patterns at play and understand how the pieces fit together.

When we understand the foundation of healthy relationships, there is a simple way to build relationships that thrive (both short-term and long-term).

Using the **CATR™ (pronounced "cater")** framework, I will share how you can identify if a relationship is healthy and functioning well, **OR if not**, which part is cracked and how to repair it. That is, unless that part is broken beyond repair.

It is not uncommon to have a relationship you're excited about; thus, you jump into it thinking it's going to work out well, only to find that it doesn't. (Hence, divorce, shattered friendships, and broken business relationships are normal.)

Why is this so common? I believe it is because we are not taught from an early age what it takes to create healthy relationships, how to keep them healthy, and how to repair them when cracks in the foundation start to form, before they break down completely.

The framework for building quality relationships is established in what we call **"The CATR Theory"**.

Introducing The CATR Theory™

The CATR Theory is a simple tool that gives anyone the ability to figure out what IS or IS NOT working in the relationship and what to fix to help the relationship thrive.

The CATR Theory uses a straightforward framework to clarify the relationship, the problem at hand, and, often, the solution involved in creating a strong and healthy connection. **CATR** breaks down complex situations, making them simple and clear, so that you can experience relationships filled with trust, respect, and ultimately happiness.

While the framework is simple, it is not always easy to implement because we are human. It is not always easy to stay mindful and use the tools in our tool belt to proactively address minor issues before they escalate into major problems. The more mindful and intentional we are, the easier it becomes to keep the relationship healthy and strong.

So, what is "The CATR Theory" and where did it come from?

Let's start with its origin.

The CATR Theory Origin

With decades of experience as a corporate account executive, business owner, and board member for multiple organizations, I have extensive experience in managing complex relationships, opening previously closed doors, and building meaningful connections.

The ability to understand and simplify complex issues—figuring out what went wrong and how to fix it—was a skill that I was respected for at work and was my superpower at home.

I felt confident in those skills until I adopted my son, who was around eleven years old at the time. We had a relationship for two years before the adoption was finalized and he got to come home. Once we made it through the honeymoon period, we struggled for a long time. No matter how hard I worked to help him feel seen, heard, understood, and valued, nothing seemed to resonate for him. We were in a daily push-pull that often ended in frustration, anger, and tears.

As a relationship development specialist, my extensive experience is in creating great partnerships. So I couldn't understand why, even with the help of therapists, **none of the approaches we used seemed to work—until something eventually did.** My son and I were then able to build upon what worked to create the beautiful, loving, supportive, and joyful relationship we have today.

During my son's high school years, several of his friends lived with us as their families navigated significant life challenges. As a solo parent, it was not easy to support four or more teenagers at once, each facing big life challenges.

The kids often didn't understand why they were having relationship difficulties with friends, partners, parents, teachers, and even bosses and coworkers. I became their go-to person to help them figure out what was happening and what to do about it.

I needed to distill all my expertise into a recipe so that even the younger kids could figure out for themselves what was happening in their relationships and how to address the issues that were causing the breakdowns. Hence, **The CATR Theory** framework was born.

Over time, I realized that this simple recipe, when followed, yields success in most relationships, both personally and professionally.

After seeing the **CATR** framework work for numerous personal and professional scenarios, many friends and colleagues have asked me to share this formula. In this framework, I teach people **The CATR Theory** and **"How to CATR Your Relationships"**.

What is The CATR Theory™?

The CATR Theory premise is that relationships with consistently healthy and strong Communication, Accountability, Trust, and Respect for each other will have higher levels of collaboration, satisfaction, and long-term partnership compared to relationships lacking these elements.

In the pages that follow, I will explore how these qualities work together, why they are important, and what is created when they function well and when they do not. I will also teach you how to get them back into alignment, because aligned insights matter in improving your Relational Intelligence to create High-RQ connections.

How to CATR Your Relationships™

My dear friend, radio host Delilah Rene, once told me, "There needs to be a copy of **The CATR Theory** in every home, school, university, and organization! By learning these skills, our world would be healthier and a much more positive place." Delilah would know. She has millions of listeners every night who tune in to hear her talk to them about navigating their relationships.

The process of using **The CATR Theory** as a filter to view the health of a relationship is what is referred to as "**CATR**

Your Relationships". It is the process of using the framework to identify the cracks and what to do to fix them.

I have been teaching **The CATR Theory** and how to **CATR Your Relationships** to many over the last few years and have recently come to understand the value of this concept.

The beauty of **The CATR Theory / CATR Your Relationships** is that it provides simple visuals, making it easy to understand and relatable, helping you strengthen your relationships.

Who is this book for?

This book is for anyone who wants to enhance the quality of their relationships in any area of life—at home, at work, or socially—or to simply learn how to be a better person in connection with others. This includes spouses/partners, executives/team leaders, employees, teachers, parents, and even teens navigating friendships—basically everyone.

There is a misconception that some people say, "I don't bring work home" or "I keep my personal life separate from work." The truth is, we can't entirely separate what we carry inside of us. Home impacts work, and work impacts home. Learning these skills in one area of your life will have a beneficial carryover to other areas as well.

How to use the book

Preface: Gives you the background on **The CATR Theory**

Part 1: **The CATR Theory** recipe

Part 2: **How to CATR Your Relationship** – Finding the cracks and fixing them, including examples

Part 3: Conclusion includes Summary, Assessment (questions to help you explore/heal your relationships), and Resources to help you grow.

The acronyms in this book are chosen intentionally as a memory aid to help you recall the framework and how it fits together. Examples of **The CATR Theory** in action are in Chapter 6.

As you read through the book, consider current relationships that you find challenging and analyze them through the **CATR** lens as you progress through each step.

Make notes about these relationships in the margins. Write down the qualities or aspects of the relationship that are working well, and also note the ones that aren't. Doing so helps you see patterns and identify changes that will make your relationships healthier and stronger.

You are also invited to reflect on previous relationships in your life that started out well but ultimately fell apart. Using **The CATR Theory** framework, can you see where the cracks initially formed? Can you see how it progressed to the point of breaking beyond repair?

The CATR Theory is designed to provide you with tools to support you in creating relationships for long-term success. Learning from the past to support your future, beginning now!

My purpose in sharing this framework is to help individuals and organizations transform their relationships and create a more respectful, kind, and synergistic world.

Let's explore the recipe of this framework together!

PART 1
The CATR Theory™

Introduction

Understanding relationships is not rocket science! Most relationships truly are simple! Here is the recipe:

Four Legs, One Foundation: C-A-T-R.

In relationships, there are four foundational legs at play. When the legs are strong, the relationship is strong. If, however, one leg cracks, it often causes the others to crack, and if not repaired quickly, the legs are at risk of breaking completely. Once broken, that leg may be irreparable.

The visual we use is that the **four legs of a healthy relationship are like the four legs of a sturdy table**. When the legs of the table are strong, you can stand on the table and dance. You can invite others to join you up on the table to dance with you; the table will often hold more weight than it was designed to support, yet it stays strong!

Likewise, when your relationship is strong, it will hold what it is intended to hold. A friendship or marriage will navigate the incredible highs and lows of life; a business partnership or an employer-employee relationship will handle the many uncertainties that arise in business, and so on.

If, however, the relationship is not strong, it won't take much for the relationship to fall apart. If the legs of the relationship crack, the relationship will not carry what it is designed to carry. Hence, we see so many divorces and failed business partnerships.

The Four Legs of The CATR Theory

The word CATR stands for the four essential "legs" of a strong, lasting connection: C, A, T, and **R**—each represents a pillar of strength in relationships:

- C – Communication
- A – Accountability
- T – Trust
- R – Respect

When we **CATR** our relationships, focusing on each of these legs with intention, we create the kind of connection which allows joy to flow, and yes, dancing to happen!

While relationships *can* be complicated, at their core, most are simple when we provide them with the right nourishment and support.

When you CATR Your Relationships, this simple framework makes the legs of your relationship table

very strong so that you can dance on it, and the table will hold for the reason, the season, or even your lifetime!

Foundational Tenets for CATR to work:

For **The CATR Theory** to work, three tenets must be present:

- **Intent** – Both parties must care about the relationship being a good one and have positive intent toward one another. They want the best for each other and are committed to that intention.
- **Interests/Values** – There needs to be at least some areas of shared interests or values upon which to foster connection.
- **Investment** – Both parties are willing to invest time and effort into the success of the relationship.

You won't always agree or share identical values, but what matters is that intentions are positive, not ill-willed, and that each person is willing to put in the effort to make the relationship a healthy one.

Key to Success: It is *much better* to protect the four legs from the beginning to keep the relationship as strong and healthy as possible. If you sense a crack forming, it is best to get it healed as quickly as possible. It will be well worth the time and investment.

The **CATR** framework will support most relationships, both personally and professionally, for young and old alike, and even across cultures. This framework has proven to be a timeless blueprint for success.

You only have control over yourself.

As you work on improving your part of the relationships in your life, you may realize that some relationships are worth investing more time, energy, and effort into, and watch them flourish beautifully. You only have control over yourself. If either of you is not willing or able to grow to the level the relationship requires, it may become clear that the connection is not suitable for the long term. **It may also become evident which relationships are ready to be blessed and released.**

Mental health professionals are trained to support healing after unhealthy relationships end. If you are navigating a challenging relationship and need support, please reach out to a mental health (behavioral health) professional for the mental wellness you deserve.

Relationships involving narcissism, trauma, and mental health disorders are outside the scope of this framework and may be best supported by mental health professionals. If you are in urgent need of support in the US, please call 988 for the National Mental Health and Suicide Hotline for assistance.

**Merriam-Webster Dictionary:

Definition of "irreparable" (adj): not repairable

Definition of "tenet" (noun): a principle, belief, or doctrine generally held to be true

Definition of "character" (noun): one of the attributes or features that make up and distinguish an individual

**New word: Definition of "CATR" (verb): to engage with the essential elements of a relationship: communication, accountability, trust, respect – pronounced 'cater'

Chapter 1
Communication

Author's note: If you have jumped ahead and not read the Preface and Introduction for understanding where **The CATR Theory** came from, I get it, I catch myself at times jumping into the heart of the solution too. As both provide essential context, I recommend reading them before proceeding to understand the foundational tenets which support **The CATR Theory**'s effectiveness.

The CATR Theory is a simple, effective, and memorable four-legged framework for creating healthy relationships in any area of your life. When you learn **The CATR Theory** and see the effectiveness, you will want to share it with those you love, so each of you can experience more trust and respect within your relationships, leading to more peace and partnership.

So, where do we start?

Let's start with the anchor legs, which are key to any successful relationship.

There are *two* anchor legs of any relationship. Without these two anchor legs being strong, the other legs will not develop. They can't because these two anchor legs provide the foundation to support the third and fourth legs, which evolve over time.

The first and most important anchor leg is COMMUNICATION.

Communication is the cornerstone of any relationship.

For a relationship to flourish, it is essential to consistently engage in healthy communication, especially when challenges arise.

Please read that again...healthy communication is essential AT ALL TIMES, ESPECIALLY WHEN IT IS HARD!

Think of a relationship where you've had a tough conversation and then wished you hadn't said what you did. Or they said things to you that were very harmful. Think about how hard it was to recover from the damage to your relationship.

In the heat of the moment, we tend to say and do things that we may not be able to recover from. Being mindful and intentional with healthy communication during difficult conversations protects the relationship, both in the short term and in the long term. **Be KIND!**

That doesn't mean you need to agree on everything. You can agree to disagree. It is through respectful disagreements and conflict that we are exposed to others' ideas from which we can grow and expand our knowledge and awareness. The more these tools are used, the easier it is to stay calm and be an effective communicator regardless of the situation.

As you get to know each other and develop the relationship—whether it is a friendship, romantic relationship, or even professional relationship—we learn about each other's communication styles. If we truly care about the relationship, we will take an interest in what communication style works best for each other (in-person, calling, texting, frequency, tone of voice, topics open for discussion, etc.) and make agreements to have healthy communication that works for both parties.

My son and I became family when he was about 11. We struggled with connecting in a way that would allow him to feel understood.

When I started to understand the power of communication, everything changed for us. We went from him not talking to me unless he had to, to us sharing everything—open, honest, and transparent, rooted in positivity, listening to learn, and partnership.

Creating a safe and supportive environment to explore the hard stuff, navigate the messy stuff, and celebrate the good stuff, while growing together, is more valuable than anything money can buy!

When the Communication Leg is strong, the other legs of the relationship have a chance to form.

Chapter 2
Accountability

The second anchor leg is ACCOUNTABILITY.

Accountability is **doing *what* you say you will do, *when* you say you will do it—and *doing it well*!**

In nearly all relationships, there will be agreements on how to support one another and nurture the relationship. These agreements take the form of the accountable actions we commit to.

The following are examples of relationship agreements:

> **Friendship:** We agree to respond to each other's communication promptly, and we also agree to show up and be supportive when the other is in need.

> **Roommates:** One agrees to cook, another agrees to do the dishes, and the third agrees to take out the garbage. All agree to pay their portion of the rent on a specific date.

> **Spouses:** One makes plans for a date while the other takes care of the pets or picks up the kids. One is supportive while the other pursues their passion.

> **Employer/Employee:** The employer agrees to provide a healthy work environment and pay the employee "X amount" on "X date" for the services being done. The employee agrees to arrive on time, perform the job well, and engage professionally.

Pause for a moment and consider a relationship you're in and the agreements you've made with each other. Now think of another relationship and the different agreements you have. Have the agreements been discussed and agreed upon, or are they just assumed?

For any relationship to be strong, you need to be able to count on each other to show up and follow through with what was agreed upon by the scheduled completion time. Occasionally, aspects can be renegotiated; however, such renegotiations should be rare for your partner to rely on you to do what you say you will, and vice versa.

Some of the biggest challenges in relationships are:

1. **Many of these agreements are never discussed.** As a result, the parties involved may have different expectations for what those unwritten agreements are.

2. **Lack of follow-through.** When follow-through does not occur, the other person cannot trust that you will consistently do what you say you will. Thus, instead, they begin to trust that you WILL NOT do what you commit to.

3. If someone is not fully vested in the relationship, **they often don't give a quality effort**. Thus, their partner cannot count on the agreed action to be done well.

4. Agreements may focus on BOTH **actions** AND *how both parties will communicate* with each other. Examples include:
   a. Tone of voice
   b. Words used (being kind/patient, swearing/or not, letting go of judgment, etc.)
   c. Topics open for discussion (including accepting the areas in which you agree to disagree and being respectful of each other's perspectives)
   d. Discussing and respecting boundaries

By not discussing these areas, the relationship is not being set up for success. Likewise, if these areas have been discussed and both parties are not being accountable to their partner, this leg of the relationship is at risk of breaking down. The sayings "Being pecked to death by ducks" or "Death by a thousand paper cuts" come to mind. Little by little, it erodes this leg if people are not being accountable to each other.

Values – Impact on Actions

Within this leg, core values matter because the actions each person chooses may not align with the others' core values. If the actions are ideologically opposed to the values, character, and boundaries for acceptability of the partner, the relationship may not be sustainable.

Example:

When my son first came to the US, we would do our household chores every Saturday. It took an hour or two. The first few months it was new and exciting, though after a while, there was pushback. In looking back through the CATR lens, I can see now where our values had an impact.

One of my core values is personal responsibility, while his primary core value is freedom. Even though personal responsibility comes naturally and is a lower core value for him, freedom supersedes it.

Thus, the Accountability Leg of the relationship suffered because it was not in alignment for both of us, as he felt our family agreement was not allowing him the freedom he had earned through being personally responsible in other areas.

By meeting in the middle to find a solution, this issue was resolved. We had a common core value that we could build upon to meet his primary need.

Once we adjusted the family agreement to allow him to complete his chores on his own terms by the agreed-upon time, it met both of our core values: his for freedom, and mine for being responsible to our family's needs and keeping one's word.

We both completed our chores on Saturday, and everyone was happy.

In today's charged environment, where it seems that we often are at odds with each other, and sometimes it appears that we do not have any shared core values. However, it may be that we have similar values, just expressed differently. There may also be a different order of priority for what is most valuable to each other (see the example above with my son).

The more core values (and common interests) are shared in a relationship, the easier it is to find common ground, both from points of connection and ways to meet in the middle on solutions. When people are aligned, it is easier for movement to flow and for follow-through to occur. Finding middle ground where both parties' needs can be met significantly strengthens the connection and often increases our willingness to show up for ourselves and our commitment to the other person.

Accountability for both words and actions is critical for relationships to survive and ideally, ultimately thrive.

When you are both consistent and reliable in healthy communication *and* your actions, the opportunity exists for the third leg to develop.

Definition of "accountable" (adj): subject to giving an account: answerable

Definition of "supersedes" (verb): to displace in favor of another

Chapter 3

Trust

When the first two legs of the relationship— COMMUNICATION and ACCOUNTABILITY—are strong, the third leg of the relationship, TRUST, begins to form.

When communication between parties is consistently healthy, even if you disagree with the other person, you can count on each person to share their truth honestly, supportive of healthy dialogue that is exploratory in nature. Even if you don't always agree, you can trust that what is communicated is their authentic truth, and you both will show care for each other's humanity.

Safe Space for Connection

Once the relationship begins to develop, and you see evidence of the other person's intentions. Over time, if there is consistent evidence that you both care for the well-being of each other and the intentions for each other are good (not ill-willed), you can begin to trust that you both have good intent for each other.

When we know the other person cares for our well-being, we can create a safe space together to be vulnerable and explore hard topics. In healthy relationships, we care for each other even when having difficult conversations. There can be an understanding that even if we disagree, we hold no ill will toward the other person and wish the best for each other.

As we grow together, we need to trust that we are supported in navigating the wholeness of our humanness. That we will not be attacked when we fall short of perfection, and we are in partnership, holding each other accountable to work through situations and become better.

Consistency of Actions

Likewise, when both parties **are consistently accountable** for the actions they have agreed to, confidence develops that you can depend on each other to perform well in the partnership. Trust begins to form when the other person is perceived as both reliable and of integrity.

Over time, as the relationship navigates its ups and downs, with both parties showing up in a supportive and engaging way through their healthy communication and accountable actions, the Trust Leg continues to strengthen, allowing for the fourth and final leg to develop.

> Definition of "exploratory" (adj): of, relating to, or being exploration

When TRUST is broken, what do you do?

When TRUST is broken, either one or both of the first two legs are cracked or broken. Evaluate whether it was the Communication Leg or the Accountability Leg that was impacted and why. Focus on what it will take to make that leg strong again.

Example:

The moment I realized there was something to this framework, my son, Osei (pronounced "oh-say"), wanted to walk to the high school to watch a ball game with a group of friends. I agreed as long as they were back by curfew. They walked in right on time, and when I asked how it went, J said, "You would have been so proud of Osei!" T (one of the other boys) really wanted to hang out with the girls, and Osei said, "T, do what you want. I am not going to break my mom's trust, because if I do, it takes a long time to repair. It's not worth it." So, with that, they made it back on time, with T in tow.

It was in that moment that I knew our CATR talks were sinking in, that there was something to the framework, and it was working.

He understood that if the Trust Leg was cracked due to his choice, he would need to put effort into repairing it. It was more important for him to protect and keep our relationship strong, letting me know I can count on him to keep his word.

This was also the moment I realized he was teaching the others the framework as well.

Repairing trust takes time, energy, effort, consistency, and commitment. A lot of work! It takes addressing the issue, taking ownership, and accountability. There may have been factors that contributed to the situation or actions that impacted trust. However, if you are the offending party who broke your partner's trust, you don't get to be the victim. Take responsibility for the choice or action that was made, make amends, and strive for consistency in repairing the first two legs.

Sometimes it is not clear what we did that broke the trust. When that happens, it may be difficult to take responsibility (when it is not clear what you are taking responsibility for). Run the scenario through the CATR framework and it may become clear.

Example:

Recently, I have had two friendships go through rough patches. In both situations, I understood my friends wanted my support, so I gave it. And in both situations, I received immediate strong feedback that the support given did not work for them.

For an extended period of time, I felt like I was the victim. My interpretation was that I was asked for support, and I gave it. I made time, despite everything I had going on, to ensure I was supportive. Now, it felt like I was being attacked. I didn't understand what I did.

Once I ran it through the CATR framework, it seemed clear.

While I was honest, open, transparent, and accepting of the situation, in both situations I was navigating other significant life challenges. Thus, I was not as patient, kind, and compassionate as I usually would have been. As a result, it didn't feel respectful or thoughtful to them.

In such situations, I can either stay stuck in needing to "be right", or I can focus on the value of our relationship and all that we have been through together to get out of being stuck. I can take the feedback and see patterns at play to grow (both for myself and for what is or is not working well in the relationship) and make adjustments.

After speaking with them, they did not want my feedback at the time; they only wanted me to be present and listen. We also discussed that a pattern emerges when I am overextended (short, direct vs. patient, thoughtful), and that this pattern of communication does not work for either of them. In the process, I broke their trust in providing a safe space for reflection. It is something I continue to work on.

I also recognized that a mirror seemed to form, in which we both had a similar experience of the other, and we did not experience each other as our usual kind and compassionate selves.

I also recognized that I need more grace when I fall short of my usual positive self. I often extend grace to others, and I deserve that kindness and compassion as well when I am in my humanness.

Extending grace and kindness, validating hurt feelings, taking ownership, and helping each other be heard, seen, understood, and valued will strengthen the friendship.

It is also an opportunity to step back and evaluate whether we need to give each other space for the relationship to breathe. Taking a break is not necessarily the same as breaking up.

If there were issues at play before the trust was broken, address the specific trust situation at hand, then also address the issues that led to the action that broke the trust. This often requires both parties to work together to repair the relationship.

Sometimes it is both parties who contribute to the crack in the **Communication Leg** by speaking disrespectfully to each other. Thus, neither party feels safe. If the **Communication Leg** is cracked, then the **Trust Leg** is going to be cracked as well. In this case, there needs to be agreements in place to prioritize healthy communication. It is then both parties' responsibility to contribute to healing that leg for the other legs to be repaired as well. All three legs will be at play: Communication, Accountability, and Trust.

Example:

When a loved one broke up with their significant other over infidelity, there was a natural reaction to assign blame and be a victim of the situation. Not taking ownership of your part in what created the problem does not support growth.

Yes, infidelity occurred, though if the relationship had been healthy and strong from the beginning, AND there was both a commitment and a priority by both parties to keep the relationship strong, there is less likelihood that the relationship would break down. When the legs are already cracked, it does not take much for them to break completely.

The fidelity issue is one issue; the other contributing factors are another issue. When both parties take ownership of their contributing part(s) rather than just pointing to the other party, there may be a chance to repair, grow, and strengthen the relationship.

If there are cracks in the Trust Leg of the relationship, get them fixed so you don't have to work so hard to repair it.

When the first three legs are strong, the environment is set for the fourth leg to grow.

Chapter 4
Respect

Definition of respect (noun):

1: a relation or reference to a particular thing or situation

2: an act of giving particular attention: consideration
Definition of respect (verb):

1: to consider worthy of high regard: esteem

When people show up consistently in a positive way for each other, and the first three legs— COMMUNICATION, ACCOUNTABIL-ITY, and TRUST—are strong, over time the fourth and final leg develops: RESPECT for one another!

When people truly respect one another, they will hold each other in high esteem (high value), and loyalty develops. **People will be there to support those they respect and are loyal to, as long as it does not violate their core**

values, and what is asked aligns with what the person is willing and able to give, even if it is inconvenient. In these instances, the effort is made out of respect for one another.

Sometimes showing respect involves holding each other accountable. Learning how to hold that accountability in a healthy way is a valuable skill. Sometimes accountability is maintained through hard conversations. However, even in hard conversations, we can set boundaries rooted in kindness and compassion rather than being unkind.

What Respect Looks Like

When we respect another person, we will take extra care of them.

If someone I respect is in urgent need, they can call me at any time of the day or night, and I will do my best to support them and help them navigate the situation. It doesn't mean that I will rescue them from accountability for whatever got them into the problem. I will help them work through the situation, accept responsibility, and empower them to grow as needed.

My son and I continually CATR our relationship. As a result, our partnership has become so strong that no matter what happens, we will be there for each other. At times, there will be conversations about lessons learned from the experience and about accountability, which can be uncomfortable yet necessary for growth.

The more we consistently show up for each other in a positive and healthy way (even if one of us is upset about something), the more we know it is a safe space for connection and support.

Because the connection and support are so strong, we know that when we challenge each other to grow, it reinforces that we have good intent for one another, and it inspires us to always do better for ourselves and for each other.

From Silos to Collaboration

Likewise, using the CATR framework at work, we have taken siloed competitive teams and helped them to become teams rooted in partnership, trust, and respect. Learning how to **CATR Your Relationships** is truly transformative, both personally and professionally.

When we respect others, they don't need to be present for us to support what benefits them because we care about the relationship and have good intentions for each other. We aim to be supportive and help one another succeed. It's important that when we assist each other, we do so without causing harm to ourselves or others in the process.

The CATR Theory provides people with the tools to move from dysfunction to partnership and collaboration. The more you use it, the stronger your relationship foundation becomes, so that you can dance in the space of healthy connection and partnership, which leads to more peace, happiness, and joy.

PART 2
CATR in Action

Chapter 5
CATR IT!
How to CATR Your Relationship: Finding the cracks and fixing them!

An essential aspect of healthy relationships is clarifying the areas of partnership so that both people are on the same page. Then focus on **what is working in the partnership** to build a strengths-based foundation of connection.

Start with the **Foundational Tenets**. Check to see if all the parties involved are committed to having a healthy relationship and have **good Intent**, have **shared Interests/Values**, and **are Invested** in making an effort for the success of the relationship.

Example:

Co-parents who have allowed a dysfunctional relationship to develop over time. If both parties are committed to being in a relationship for the sake of the children (or even for their own mental health), then they may need to agree to work on the relationship.

By using the **CATR** approach to uncover specific areas needing support, they can then work on healing those key areas.

For any relationship, once you have identified an issue causing a crack, connect with your partner and address how to fix that area kindly and respectfully, rooted in partnership.

How to find the crack(s):

It is easiest to **CATR Your Relationship** by starting at the fourth leg and working backward—ask yourself the following questions:

1. **Leg 4: Do I RESPECT this person?** If there is an aspect you don't respect, we need to look at Leg 3: TRUST.

2. **Leg 3: What is the aspect of the person I don't TRUST?** Look deeper at what the area is that you don't trust. Is it that you don't feel safe and supported, or something else? The answer will be most likely found in Leg 2: ACCOUNTABILITY.

3. **Leg 2: What is the aspect of ACCOUNTABILITY that is at play?** Are the actions not being followed through as agreed upon, or what is the aspect(s) impacting the experience? If it is action-oriented, make an agreement around the aspect at play. (Agreements should include both outcomes—what can be expected if the agreement is kept, and what can be expected when the agreement is NOT kept.) If it is an issue with communication, the answer will most likely be found in Leg 1: COMMUNICATION.

4. **Leg 1: Evaluate the health of the COMMUNICATION Leg.** We call it the **HOT ART of Communication™** which evaluates HOW and WHAT to communicate for the communication to be healthy and strong.

Since *many* relationship issues are rooted in aspects of communication, let's go deeper into that leg to understand how to make it as strong as possible.

CATR IT! COMMUNICATION

Fortifying the Cornerstone

Definition of "fortifying" (verb): to make strong

Definition of "cornerstone" (noun): a basic element : FOUNDATION

As mentioned at the beginning, communication is the cornerstone of any relationship. Thus, understanding the components of healthy communication is key to making the foundation as strong as possible.

Although WHAT is communicated, WHEN it is communicated, and HOW it is communicated are essential. The WHY is easy: because you care about the relationship and are vested in keeping it healthy and strong.

In any relationship, the importance of the **HOT ART of Communication** cannot be overstated, as it forms the foundational leg of the connection.

- **H**onest
- **O**pen
- **T**ransparent

- **A**ccepting with Agreements
- **R**espectful in Tone
- **T**houghtful

We call this the **HOT ART of Communication**.

If either person in the relationship is not fully honest, not willing to communicate, cutting corners on being entirely truthful, their words are not in alignment with their actions, they are disrespectful in words or tone, unkind in their delivery, or each is constantly trying to change the other...each one of these types of scenarios will chip away at the strength of the cornerstone of their relationship which is the **Communication Leg**. Without that leg being strong, it impacts the **Accountability, Trust, and Respect Legs,** which may not form well.

To heal this: Create agreements with each other around committing to use the **HOT ART of Communication**. When making agreements, build in accountability, which means build into the agreement "When we keep this agreement, then _____." And "If the agreement is not kept, then_____." Consequences of agreements are not rewards or punishments, they are just the results of whether the agreement was kept...or not.

An example here might be that "We agree to commit to using communication with each other that is fully honest, open, transparent, accepting with agreements, respectful in tone, and thoughtful. When we keep this agreement, we will acknowledge the great qualities we appreciate in each other which took place in that moment; i.e., I appreciate your partnership, vulnerability, and integrity that you kept the agreement even if it may not have been easy. When we do not keep this agreement, we need to take a pause and reset, then get back in alignment with what we have agreed to."

If the agreement keeps getting broken by one party, they may need to make amends to the other party.

Ego vs. Partnership

When we are in disagreements with our partner (spouse, friend, co-worker, etc.) it is good to do a check-in. **Is it more important for me to be right or is the relationship more important?** This is important when we consider that each person has a unique viewpoint based on their lived experiences and the data they believe to be factual. Sometimes it is valuable to hold your position, though many times it is the little things that keep us apart.

When ego is at play and we feel a need to be "right for the sake of being right", then the relationship pays the toll.

When we set aside our ego and commit to the partnership, we can often grow as a result. When both parties are committed to the relationship, such that they learn to set aside their ego for the little things, then when it comes to the bigger, essential issues, there is more bandwidth to explore and give grace for working together, because all the little things are not filling up that space and breaking down the relationship.

It is essential to create a safe space for exploring topics and to truly *listen to learn* about the other person's thoughts and feelings. It is then that we can learn from each other and grow together. Without a safe space for connection, the relationship is not a healthy one.

Differing Viewpoints: Curious vs. Furious

I have people I love who hold different political views from mine. Inherently, what we have in common is that we are *all* very good people. We are kind, compassionate, generous, respectful, thoughtful, and well-intentioned.

And we see the role of such things as government differently. When we communicate, we explore our areas of difference respectfully, and if energy escalates as it does on occasion, by seeking to **"be curious over furious"**, we show each other that we care deeply about one another and our relationship. Sometimes we agree to keep certain topics off limits to protect the relationship. We can agree to disagree, while finding other areas to grow together and learn from each other vs. becoming positioned and siloed.

Communication/Accountability/Trust/Respect: In this situation, by focusing on WHAT is communicated and HOW it is communicated (using **HOT ART**) and being accountable for both parties staying respectful in times of disagreement, **it creates trust that both people care about each other AND the relationship and will do the work necessary to protect the connection.** Over time, this fosters a deep respect for the many areas on which we agree.

Ideological Differences

For some people with ideological differences, they may initially perceive that the only things they have in common are their familial relationship or their shared work. This may or may not be enough to establish a solid foundation for a relationship. By exploring other topics, you might discover that you have more in common than you initially believed— perhaps a love of family, shared interests, or similar life experiences. It's crucial to identify areas on which you can build the relationship's foundation and to maintain agreements around aspects on which you agree to disagree. Otherwise, a healthy relationship may struggle to survive due to conflicting core values.

If the core values of the parties are not aligned, the other areas of common interest may not be enough to sustain the relationship. It may then be time to examine your core values and determine whether they are healthy for yourself, others, and the world. If they are not healthy, it might be time to re-evaluate the lens through which you see the world.

When we observe multiple aspects in communication (i.e., the HOT ART aspects), if we perform well in several areas, those will support the whole structure even if one or two aspects become damaged. The impacted part of the relationship will still hold together while that specific area is being repaired.

Example:

There are times when I have many competing pressures and don't speak as thoughtfully to my son as I normally do, or do not show the compassion he needs in the moment. While it damages the relationship in the moment, he knows I am consistently honest, open, transparent, accepting, kind, compassionate, forgiving, loving, generous, etc. Thus, if I have a human moment where I don't show up as my best, he shows me grace and holds the space for me to make amends and clean up my mistake. (I do the same for him in the areas he is working on as well.)

Showing grace for each other does not excuse the wrongdoing; it does factor in the wholeness of our humanness. Some days we show up better than others. Perfection is not attainable in human form.

It is important that I take ownership and make things right with him. And it is also important that I stay mindful and do my best not to repeat the mistake. I want to treat him with the kindness and compassion he deserves. We are both human and are still evolving; thus, we have not perfected this yet. As long as we truly put effort into treating each other in a healthy way, we will continue to extend grace and partnership as we grow individually and collectively.

In a scenario such as this, it is much more difficult to crack/break the whole leg because the structure of the **Communication Leg** is strong.

To make this leg extra strong, wrap the communication in the **power of positivity** (refrain from negativity) and **listen to learn** (vs. listening to respond), both of which will make the communication exponentially powerful.

Learning how to CATR Your Relationship to fortify the Communication Leg as much as possible, you are setting up the relationship for success! This is the cornerstone of your relationship, which is the leg upon which the rest of the relationship is built. CATR IT at every opportunity! For most relationships, it will be the best investment you can make!

Chapter 6
Examples

Here are some examples of **The CATR Theory** in action:

Romantic Relationship

T came to me asking for support in a romantic relationship quandary. He and the girl he was seeing were dealing with jealousy and insecurity, leading to multiple fights with raised voices. So, we started at the beginning using the **CATR** framework to see where the issue causing the problem was.

What has been the communication regarding the agreements you have with each other? They didn't have clear agreements about whether they were seeing each other exclusively or not. Without clear agreements, it is challenging to ensure that actions align with each other's expectations. Additionally, the way they communicated with each other was not kind, thoughtful, considerate, or respectful. How can you build trust or respect for each other if you are not creating a safe space for engagement? You can't!

Healthy communication is the foundation for any relationship! Period! Full stop!

Which legs are at play?

All four—
Communication/Accountability/Trust/Respect:

In **T**'s situation, clarifying communication helped establish clear boundaries for their accountability, leading to increased trust and respect for each other and the relationship. Once they were on the same page and agreed to communicate in healthy and respectful ways, it became easier to build and maintain trust and respect for one another.

Family

M and **A** are siblings with very different personalities who approach the world in distinct ways. **A** is rational and linear in her approach to understanding and engaging with situations. **M** is very creative, beautifully sentimental, and nonlinear in how she sees and interacts in the world. For years, they have found it difficult to communicate effectively, often leaving engagements frustrated, not feeling understood, and hopeless regarding how they could ever engage in healthy and effective ways. In these instances, neither felt psychologically safe; thus, they could not trust that they would have a positive interaction, and as a result, it was hard for them to respect each other.

Since they have started using the **CATR** framework, they now understand and respect each other's unique differences, which are actually each other's superpowers. Now, when they engage with each other, they do their best to be thoughtful of how the other person sees and experiences things. **M** will do her best to present her ideas to **A** in a more linear way, and **A** shows more patience, grace, and compassion for how she approaches a conversation with **M**.

Both make an effort to let go of the "need to be right" when communicating. They now experience more partnership and joy in their relationship and enjoy each other regularly.

Communication/Trust/Respect: By focusing on accepting each other's differences and being thoughtful of the other's experience, they are protecting the Communication Leg. They are both committed to speaking respectfully to each other, which helps create a psychologically safe space for them to work through any issues that arise. As a result of consistency, they now trust that the space to engage is safe and respectful, which has helped them to be graceful with each other when they have an off day. They now have respect for each other and will show up for each other vs. avoid engagement. They are now able to dance together on the table of their relationship!

Repairing Breaks – Professional

When we enter into a work engagement, specific agreements are made upon entering the employment or partnership relationship. Such agreements may include that the employer will provide a safe working environment and clearly outline what work is to be completed by when, and what pay/benefits will be provided and how. In return, the employee agrees to show up on time, do the agreed-upon work well, behave in a professional manner, etc. Sometimes there are areas of agreement that need to be clarified.

J has heard me describe how to **CATR** relationships for several years. Thus, there are times when she calls me for assistance with figuring out what happened and how to fix a situation at work. A recent scenario involved a coworker raising their voice and speaking disrespectfully to her. As a result, she didn't feel safe or respected. In this situation, the **Communication, Accountability, Trust,** and **Respect** legs were all cracked by the actions of the coworker. Because this scenario had played out more than a couple of times, all four of the legs were not only cracked, they were also broken.

As we unpacked where the breakdown occurred and looked closer at the situation, we discovered something interesting. In this case, she worked on a production line which had steps laid out for every action and contingency in their Standard Operating Procedures (SOP) manual. During a recent SOP update, she realized there was a step missing in the directions given for what needed to happen in her role. She had been there for a long time and knew the step was important for quality assurance, though it was no longer listed in the SOP manual. As a result of the missing step, there was no longer consistency within the team.

Enforcement was no longer clear, even though it was the right thing to do. So each time she protected the quality of the product, it became a point of contention among the team. (This impacted both the Communication and Accountability [Action] Legs. The communication was not entirely clear; therefore, the action she performed did not meet the expectations of her coworkers. When challenged on it, the coworkers agreed her actions were correct, and the SOP needed to be updated.)

A couple of things needed to happen to repair the cracks:

1. **Accountability:** The SOP manual was updated to accurately reflect all steps to be taken so everyone's actions could then align with expectations.
2. **Communication/Accountability/Trust/Respect:** J communicated with her coworkers, explaining the impact of the way they had been speaking to her and the results. She created a boundary for healthy communication and was open in dialogue with both

HR and her supervisor about what healthy communication would entail. The supervisor, wanting to support her experience, put support systems in place. (These steps by the supervisor helped to strengthen all four legs: He communicated and took action, which in turn helped to repair the trust within the team and increased her respect for the organization.)

This is a case where it's not always what happens, it's how we respond to what happens, which can make or break a situation.

How Respect Impacts Actions

For several years, I was president of my HOA. During that time, I knew the importance of healthy communication and accountability in building trust and ultimately respect. It was vital for me always to maintain integrity and show respect for those with whom I disagreed on policy. While most everyone got along very well and we built a healthy, trusting, and respectful community, there were a few who never got along. No matter how hard the board tried, they seemed focused on breaking the community down due to self-serving interests rather than working together to find solutions in the best interest of everyone. Nothing we could do seemed to appease the few who refused to strengthen the community.

So how do we address this issue?

Foundational Tenet: All parties must be interested in fostering a healthy relationship. In this case, it is not a matter of giving up on the relationship; it is a choice to become "curious over furious," learning more about the other person's interests, values, and ultimate goals, while thinking outside the box for solutions.

Communication/Accountability/Trust/Respect:
By focusing on communication and seeking to understand everyone's perspective, fears, values, and what mattered to them, we fostered a working trust and mutual respect that

was rooted in accountability and agreements on how disagreements would be handled. In this case, all four legs were at play. We were able to transform a dysfunctional community into a functional one, working together in the best interests of everyone.

There are so many examples which could be shared here, though the pattern is the same. When there is an issue in a relationship, use **The CATR Theory** framework to **"CATR Your Relationship"** to check where the cracks are and repair them.

PART 3
Conclusion

Chapter 7
Conclusion

We are navigating big challenges in our world at this time. It will take us doing things differently to bridge the divides and increase healing and harmony.

It starts with each of us and how we show up in our connection with others, growing in our Relational Intelligence (RQ).

The goal of this book is to help us all experience more peace and harmony in our world. It doesn't have to be hard when we understand the recipe.

When learning to "**CATR Your Relationships**", we can identify which aspects are functioning well and which areas are at risk of cracking or breaking. If the relationship is valuable to you, it may be worth the time and investment to strengthen that area.

If you struggle to create healthy relationships, I hope this will help you see things more clearly and provide you with the tools to make lasting, positive changes in your life, allowing you to dance in the joy of connection with the people you care about.

For people to feel seen, heard, understood, and valued, we must focus on the positive aspects of any moment. Focusing on the positive vs. the challenges before us is a game-changer.

In this moment, I want you to know that you are seen and valued. I want to acknowledge a bit of what is great about you. If you have read this far, I see the greatness of your curiosity and interest in personal growth.

May you find the tools you need within these pages to practice using **The CATR Theory** to support your relationships, so you can dance in the joy of healthy connections for years to come!

Using these tools, Osei and I have transformed our relationship. For over a decade, our relationship has been built on trust, respect, teamwork, and partnership, regardless of the challenges we face. We are each other's biggest cheerleaders, and we constantly hold each other accountable for how we show up in the world.

Using **The CATR Theory**, I have seen this transformation in many other relationships as well.

I pray this gift will help you, your loved ones, and your colleagues dance on the tables of high-quality relationships by utilizing **The CATR Theory** to **CATR Your Relationships**.

Let's work together to help our world heal, one relationship at a time. By coming together and fixing the cracks, we can positively transform unhealthy family environments and work culture to be grounded in trust and respect.

The final two chapters are a summary of **The CATR Theory**, and resources to support your journey ahead. Wishing you blessings as you and your loved ones grow together in partnership.

Chapter 8
Summary

The **CATR Theory** premise is that relationships with consistently healthy and strong COMMUNICATION, ACCOUNTABILITY, TRUST, and RESPECT have higher levels of collaboration, satisfaction, and long-term partnership compared to relationships lacking these elements.

The **CATR Theory** encompasses the qualities needed for High-Relationship Intelligence (High-RQ)** interactions.

For **The CATR Theory** to work, three **Foundational Tenets** must be present:

- **Intent** – Both parties must care about the relationship being a good one and have positive intent toward one another. They want the best for each other and are committed to that intention.
- **Interests/Values** – There needs to be at least some areas of shared interests or values upon which to foster connection.

- **Investment** – Both parties are willing to invest time and effort into the success of the relationship.

CATR Framework

The anchor leg in any relationship is **COMMUNICATION**. Communication that is honest, open, transparent, accepting with agreements, respectful in tone, and thoughtful, rooted in positivity, and where each person truly listens to learn about their partner so the partner to feels seen, heard, understood, and valued.

The second most important leg in any relationship is **ACCOUNTABILITY.** Accountability in both how both parties communicate with one another and the actions each person is responsible for in the relationship. Regarding actions, both parties need to do what they have committed to doing by the agreed-upon time. Renegotiation can only take place once or twice on an issue, or they cannot be relied upon to keep their word. When the Communication and Accountability Legs are consistently strong, the third leg, **TRUST**, will develop.

When the third leg, **TRUST**, develops, the parties do not always need to agree on everything. They can agree to disagree, though there has been consistently healthy communication, which helps each other feel safe while exploring topics. There is also trust that has developed that both parties will show up and do what they agree to do by the time they agree to do it. Trust develops both ways—trust that each party will show up well or trust that they *will not* show up well. If the Trust Leg develops in a healthy way to be consistently strong in both healthy communication and consistently accountable, then the fourth leg, RESPECT, grows.

When the fourth leg, **RESPECT**, is strong, both parties will have each other's back through both the good times and hard times, as long as what is being asked of them does not violate their core values and is not beyond what they are able or willing to give. They will be there for each other because they want the best for each other, and they want to see each other succeed.

When these four legs are healthy and strong, the relationship will grow and evolve in partnership.

Assessing the Communication Leg

Think about a relationship **where the communication style feels positive and healthy,** and ask yourself:

1. Do I feel seen, heard, understood, and valued? Has my partner expressed that they do/do not feel seen, heard, understood, and valued?

2. Do I feel uplifted and cared about after most interactions?

3. What is it about the type of communication I share with that person that feels good to me? (Make a mental note or write it in the margins here.)

Now, consider a relationship you have **where the type of communication doesn't work for you** and ask yourself:

1. Is there too much or too little information shared?

2. What about the communication with this person doesn't feel good?

3. Do I feel like I am getting the whole picture, or do I have challenges trusting what I am being told?

4. Are the words used kind, compassionate, and thoughtful, or does the tone convey a sense of disrespect?

Assessing the Accountability Leg

Think about a relationship **where you know you can count on that person, and they can count on you,** and ask yourself:

1. What are the indicators that tell me this person is accountable? Is it in the form of actions, communication, or both?

2. What are some of the examples of how they have shown me I can count on them for quality engagement and timely follow-through?

3. How does this make me feel knowing that I can count on them?

4. Can they count on me to the same degree?

Now consider a relationship in which **you are experiencing conflict around accountability** and ask yourself:

1. Is the issue related to communication or actions?

2. Are there clear agreements that have been discussed in the areas of concern? Or are there assumptions that have never been clarified?

3. Do the agreements include both ends of the spectrum (i.e., When the agreement is kept _____ happens, and if the agreement is not kept _____ happens.) Are you following through on what the agreements are?

**Reminder: Boundaries can be held in kindness vs. anger and resentment. Also, some of the most powerful agreements are brief and to the point, something to interrupt the pattern, not needing to be long and drawn out.

4. Consider if core values may influence why you each feel strongly, keeping you positioned and not in harmony.

- Think about what some of your core values are.
- Then think about your partner and what some of their core values are (or seem to be).
- Now consider a sticking point in your relationship that comes to mind. What are the core values at play for each of you in this situation?
- Look at the problem from your partner's point of view. Is there a way to approach the situation differently that could be in alignment with both of your core values being met?

- Discuss with your partner. Please do not assume that you are correct about what is important to them. Ask if what you perceive is accurate, and listen to learn what matters to them.
- Adjust your new insight based on any new information.
- See if you both can work together to create a win-win, where each other's needs are being met, and the problem is resolved.

If each other's values are at least somewhat aligned, the foundation of the relationship has a chance to grow.

Assessing the Trust Leg

Think about a relationship **where you have strong trust in each other**. Ask yourself:

1. What do I trust about the relationship?
2. Think about how that trust was built over time. What contributed to the trust becoming strong?
3. What does that trust provide for me?

Now consider a relationship **where you do not trust the person**. Is the issue related to communication or accountability in actions?

Trust in Communication:

1. Do you trust that you are safe to open up, be authentically you, and be vulnerable?

2. Do you provide a safe space for your partner? How can this area be improved?

3. How do you and your partner show up for each other in hard conversations?

4. Do you trust that you both will be consistently kind and compassionate, especially during hard conversations?

5. Do you trust that the agreements will be kept for what and how you have agreed to communicate with each other?

Trust in Actions:

1 Do you trust that your partner will consistently follow-through in what they have agreed to do? How consistent are you in your follow-through?

2 For each of you, is the follow-through timely, and are the results of high quality, or are they consistently lacking?

3 When you make agreements, do you trust the agreements will be upheld by both of you?

Assessing the Respect Leg

1. Do you respect the person you are in a relationship with?

2. Are you willing to support them when they are in need, even if it is not convenient?

3. Do they show up for you when you are in need, even if it is not convenient?

4. If the answer is no to any of these first three questions, consider what is impacting your willingness to extend yourself to each other.

Now that you understand what **is working** and what **is not working** in each leg of the relationship, let's put into practice how to **CATR Your Relationships™**.

As you navigate this time in our world, there are ways you can make it a healthier and more enjoyable experience. **The CATR Theory™** provides you with tools to create long-lasting, high-quality relationships even with people you may not always agree with.

Relationships are a part of the roller coaster of life. When you learn to **CATR Your Relationships™**, you gain high relationally intelligent tools to help repair them when minor cracks happen, keeping small issues manageable.

Not sure what is going on...**CATR IT™!** You might be surprised how quickly you both can get back to your happy place.

You are worthy of dancing on the tables of fulfilling, high-quality relationships. Now you have the tools and knowledge to make it happen!

Chapter 9
CATR Resources

Below are resources to help you strengthen your relationships. The items listed are in order of the most relevant for implementation of The CATR Theory to heal our world at home and at work.

The CATR Theory™ – Book Club Guide

To host a book club discussion on **The CATR Theory™** - access the book club guide at:

www.AlignedInsightsMatter.com/Resources

Between Us™ – Reflections to Strengthen Relationships (card game)

This is a card game I have developed along with my son, Osei Thibert, who is now a Certified Couple's Coach. The game is designed to support conversations with your partner to reveal insights in the areas of Communication, Actions, Trust, Respect, Patience, and Reassurance, and strengthen your relationship.

Link to **Between Us™** card game: www.BuiltByOT.com

AIM – Aligned Insights Matter

Information on Executive Coaching/Consulting for organizations using the **CATR Your Relationships™ Playbook** can be found at:

www.AlignedInsightsMatter.com

AIM² ™ – Accountability in Motion (gatherings where Aligned Insights Matter)

Gatherings can be held in any community, organization, or institution where individuals can support each other in accountability, both in communication and actions, using **The CATR Theory™** framework.

AIM² ™ – Accountability in Motion (gatherings where Aligned Insights Matter) is designed to be a safe space where those who want to uplevel their relationships can explore ways to increase their effectiveness in being accountable and in supporting others in their accountability. The carryover often positively impacts lives both personally and professionally.

For more information, visit:

www.AlignedInsightsMatter.com/Resources

CATR IT™! – Children's Book Series: coming soon

Helping children learn **The CATR Theory™** from a young age will help them develop healthy relationships throughout their lives. The series follows a group of children as they navigate their friendships. When they want to improve their friendships, they learn how to **CATR IT™** to identify where the cracks are and how to fix them.

For more information, visit:

www.AlignedInsightsMatter.com/Resources

About the Author

Laurie Thibert is a business leader, relationship specialist, and founder of Aligned Insights Matter™, where she helps organizations develop high-trust, high-performing teams. Her leadership philosophy was shaped not only in boardrooms but also in 2008 during a volunteer trip to Ghana, where she met a young boy whose parents had died. Soon, she began the journey of becoming his mom. Their journey together strengthened her belief that high-quality relationships are built when the relational fabric is strengthened.

Today, Laurie guides executives and teams to strengthen relationships, fostering trust and mutual respect—proving that when leaders lead with both head and heart, performance follows. The carryover improves personal relationships as well. Laurie is committed to helping our world thrive in vibrant and connected ways.

Laurie is passionate about contributing to the world in the areas of clean water, education initiatives, and helping children to experience loving families through foster care/adoption. She is on the board of www.WaterAccessNow.org, partners with Delilah Rene in support of projects with www.PointHope.org, and is an advocate for www.HelpUsAdopt.org. A portion of the proceeds of **The CATR Theory™** books will go to these organizations.

Ultimately, Laurie is all about making love visible at every opportunity.

A big thank you to June Dillinger for coining the term Making Love Visible© and allowing this concept to be lived and shared abundantly. www.makinglovevisible.com

Follow Laurie for more Aligned Insights here:
LinkedIn: www.linkedin.com/in/laurie-thibert

The.CATR.Theory

@the.catr.theory

@The.CATR.Theory

@The.CATR.Theory

Follow Osei for personal relationship support:

Osei Thibert

@builtbyot

@builtbyot

@builtbyot

www.ingramcontent.com/pod-product-compliance
Lightning Source LLC
Chambersburg PA
CBHW071116210326
41519CB00020B/6316